THIS U.S. GOVERNMENT BOOK BELONGS TO:

_____

_____

U.S. Government

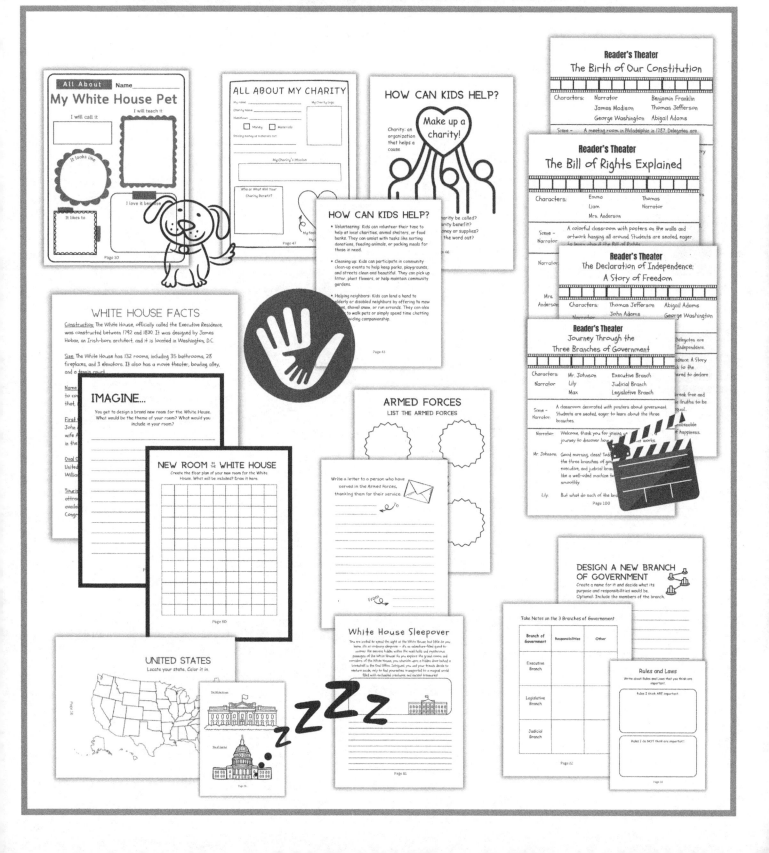

U.S.
Government

Table of Contents

Topic	Writing	Pages
Introduction to Government	Writing Activity: Locate Your State Rules & Laws	1-9
Branches of Government	Note Taking Page, Design a New Branch of Government	10-11
Executive Branch	Would you rather be President or Vice President? Presidential Pets	12-21
Legislative Branch	What interests would you want protected?	22-25
Judicial Branch	Would you rather be the judge or sitting on the supreme court?	26-30
Citizen Participation	How Kids Can Help! Make a list. Make up a charity.	31-36

Table of Contents

Table of Contents

Topic	Writing	Pages
Constitution	Freedom of Speech; What message would you want to share with the world?	37-39
Declaration of Independence	How or When Do You Show Courage?	40-42
Bill of Rights	What outrageous rules would you add to the Bill of Rights?	43-45
Pledge of Allegience	Re-Write the Pledge or Tell Why it is Important. My Pledge to Myself	46-50
Gettysburg Address	How can we make our country a better place?	51-53
Armed Forces	List the Armed Forces. Which do you think is the most important? Write a Letter	54-60

Table of Contents

Table of Contents

Table of Contents

EXPLORING U.S. GOVERNMENT

Objectives:

- Understand the basic structure and functions of the United States government.

- Identify key roles and responsibilities of government officials.

- Recognize the importance of citizen participation in democracy.

- Develop an appreciation for the principles of democracy and the rule of law.

UNDERSTANDING U.S. GOVERNMENT

What is Government?

Government is like a team of people who work together to make sure our community is safe and fair for everyone. Just like a team needs a coach to lead them, a government has leaders who make decisions to help everyone live together peacefully.

UNDERSTANDING U.S. GOVERNMENT

What is the Purpose of Government?

The purpose of government is to take care of its people and make sure everyone is treated fairly. Here are important things that government does:

- Making and Enforcing Rules: Government creates rules called laws. These laws help us know what we can and cannot do. For example, there are laws that say we have to wear seatbelts in the car to stay safe and laws that tell us not to hurt others.

- Protecting People's Rights: Government makes sure that everyone has rights. Rights are like promises that say we deserve to be treated with kindness and fairness. For example, we have the right to go to school, speak our minds, and be safe in our homes.

UNDERSTANDING U.S. GOVERNMENT

Purpose of Government Continued

- Providing Public Services: Government helps provide things that everyone needs, like schools, parks, roads, and libraries. These are called public services because they are for everyone in the community to use and enjoy.

- Keeping People Safe: Government has special people like police officers and firefighters who keep us safe. They help us when there are emergencies and make sure we can live without fear.

UNITED STATES

Locate your state. Color it in.

RULES AND LAWS

What are Rules and Laws?

- **Rules:** Rules are like guidelines that help us know how to behave and what to do in different situations. For example, in school, there are rules about raising our hands to speak and sharing toys with friends.

- **Laws:** Laws are rules made by the government. They are more serious than regular rules and everyone has to follow them. If someone breaks a law, there may be consequences, like getting a ticket or going to court.

Rules and Laws

Write about Rules and Laws that you think are important.

Rules I think ARE important:

Rules I do NOT think are important:

Rules and Laws

Write about Rules and Laws that you think are important.

Laws I think are important:

Laws I do NOT think are important:

Rules and Laws

A NEW rule I would make is...

A NEW Law I would make is...

THREE BRANCHES OF GOVERNMENT

Imagine the government is like a big tree with three branches. Each branch has its own important job to do to keep our country running smoothly. Let's explore the roles and responsibilities of each branch of government!

Just like the branches of a tree work together to make it strong, the three branches of government work together to make our country strong and fair. Each branch has its own important job, and by working together, they help keep our country safe, free, and fair for everyone.

Executive Branch
Legislative Branch
Judicial Branch

Take notes on the following page.

Take Notes on the 3 Branches of Governement

Branch of Government	Responsibilities	Other
Executive Branch		
Legislative Branch		
Judicial Branch		

EXECUTIVE BRANCH

The Executive Branch includes these important roles and responsibilities:

- Head of Government and Commander in Chief, the President: The President is like the leader of our country. Their job is to make sure the laws are being followed and to keep our country safe. They also make important decisions about things like the economy and relations with other countries.

- Commander-in-Chief: The president is the commander-in-chief of the armed forces, which means they have authority over the military. The president can make decisions about national security and defense, including deploying troops and responding to threats to our country.

EXECUTIVE BRANCH

The roles and responsibilities of the Executive Branch also include:

- The Vice President: The Vice President helps the President and takes over if the President can't do their job for some reason. They also have their own important duties, like leading special projects and helping the President make decisions.

- Enforcing Laws: The executive branch is responsible for enforcing the laws of the country. This means that the president, who is the head of the executive branch, oversees government agencies and departments that carry out laws passed by the legislative branch. State and local police forces are an example of government agencies.

EXECUTIVE BRANCH

- Diplomacy: The executive branch works with other countries. This involves negotiating treaties, making agreements, and representing the country's interests on the global level.

- Appointments: The president nominates individuals to fill key positions in the government.

- Veto Power: The president has the power to veto, or reject, bills passed by Congress.

- Most President's have owned pets and they have the responsibility to take care of their pets. If you were the president, which kind of pet would you have?

WOULD YOU RATHER...

be President or Vice President of the United States? Why?

_____

_____

_____

_____

_____

_____

_____

_____

_____

WHITE HOUSE PETS

Throughout history, several pets have lived in the White House with various presidents and their families. Here are some notable examples:

Dogs: Dogs are the most common pets in the White House. Many presidents have had dogs, including George Washington, who had several foxhounds and other breeds.

Cats: Cats have also been popular pets in the White House. Abraham Lincoln's family had several cats, including one named Tabby.

Birds: Several presidents have kept birds as pets. Thomas Jefferson had a pet mockingbird named Dick, and Andrew Jackson had a parrot named Poll.

WHITE HOUSE PETS

Horses: Some presidents have kept horses at the White House. Theodore Roosevelt, who was an avid outdoorsman, had several horses, including a pony named Algonquin for his children. Ronald Reagan had a horse named El Alamein, which was a gift from Mexican President José López Portillo.

Other Animals: Other animals that have lived in the White House include rabbits, hamsters, guinea pigs, and even an alligator, a raccoon, opossums and a flock of sheep.

WHITE HOUSE PETS

President Coolidge and his wife Grace had a variety of pets during their time in the White House, including dogs, cats, and even a bobcat. However, one of the most unusual pets was a raccoon named Rebecca.

Rebecca was a gift to the Coolidge family from a supporter in Mississippi who intended for her to be served as a meal. However, President Coolidge decided to keep her as a pet instead.

Rebecca quickly became a beloved member of the White House household and was known for her mischievous antics.

The tale of Rebecca the raccoon adds a touch of humor and warmth to the history of America's most famous residence.

All About
My White House Pet

I will call it

I will teach it

It looks like

It likes to

I love it because

My Presidential Pet

Draw your pet or your pet's home.

MY PRESIDENTIAL PET

Write a story about your presidential pet(s) living at the White House.

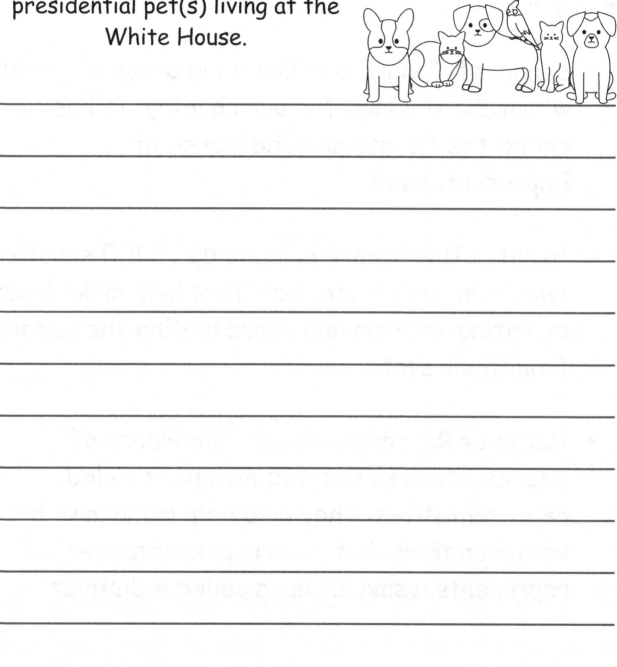

_____

_____

_____

_____

_____

_____

_____

_____

_____

_____

LEGISLATIVE BRANCH

The Legislative Branch is made up of the following groups:

- Congress: Congress is like a big group of people who make the laws for our country. It has two parts: the Senate and the House of Representatives.

- Senate: The Senate is made up of 100 senators, two from each state. Senators help make laws by voting on them and representing the people from their state.

- House of Representatives: The House of Representatives has 435 members called representatives. They also help make laws by voting on them, but each representative represents a smaller area called a district.

LEGISLATIVE BRANCH

The legislative branch plays a very important role in the government. Responsibilities include:

- Making Laws: Members, who are often called lawmakers or legislators, propose, debate, and vote on bills that can become new laws.

- Represent the People: Members of this branch are elected by the citizens to represent their interests and concerns in the government.

- Checks and Balances: The legislative branch acts as a check on the other branches of government, including the executive branch and the judicial branch. They make sure that no one branch becomes too powerful.

LEGISLATIVE BRANCH

- Budgeting and Spending: The legislative branch is responsible for approving the government's budget and overseeing how taxpayer money is spent.

- Impeachment: The legislative branch has the power to impeach, or bring charges against, government officials, including the president, for wrongdoing.

WHAT INTERESTS WOULD YOU WANT PROTECTED...

by the LEGISLATIVE branch? What interests do you have that are important to you?

_____

_____

_____

_____

_____

_____

_____

_____

_____

_____

JUDICIAL BRANCH

The judicial branch is responsible for upholding the Constitution. It includes the following group:

- The Supreme Court: The Supreme Court is like a group of judges who make sure the laws are fair and follow the rules of our country. They listen to arguments from both sides of a case and make decisions about what the laws mean and how they should be applied.

The judicial branch is responsible for the following roles:

- Interpreting Laws: The judicial branch is responsible for interpreting and applying the laws of the country. This means that judges in this branch listen to legal arguments presented in court cases and make decisions based on how they understand the law.

JUDICIAL BRANCH

- Ensuring Justice: Makes sure that justice is served by fairly resolving disputes and upholding the rights of individuals.

- Judicial Review: One important power they have is judicial review. This allows courts to review laws passed by the legislative branch and actions taken by the executive branch to make sure they are consistent with the Constitution.

- Protecting Rights: Plays a vital role in protecting the rights of citizens. Courts have the authority to hear cases involving violations of individual rights, such as freedom of speech, freedom of religion, and the right to a fair trial.

- Interpreting the Constitution: The supreme law of the land, judges analyze the Constitution making sure that the government operates within the bounds of the Constitution.

WOULD YOU RATHER BE...

the Judge or a Juror on the Supreme
Court, hearing a case at trial?

_____

_____

_____

_____

_____

_____

_____

_____

_____

BRANCHES OF GOVERNMENT

<u>Legislative Branch</u>: Responsible for making laws. It is composed of the Congress, which includes two houses: Senate and House of Representatives. Functions include:

- Drafting, debating, and passing laws.
- Overseeing the federal budget and taxation.
- Declaring war and regulating interstate and foreign commerce.
- Checking and balancing the powers of the other branches through oversight and investigation.

<u>Executive Branch</u>: Responsible for enforcing and carrying out laws. It is headed by the President of the United States. Functions include:

- Enforcing federal laws and court decisions.
- Commanding the military.
- Negotiating treaties with foreign countries..
- Appointing federal judges, ambassadors, and cabinet members.
- Vetoing or signing bills passed by Congress into law.

<u>Judicial Branch</u>: Responsible for interpreting and applying laws. It is headed by the Supreme Court of the United States. Functions include:

- Interpreting the Constitution and determining the fairness of laws.
- Resolving disputes between states and federal government.
- Serving as the highest court of appeal for cases involving federal law or constitutional issues.
- Checking the powers of the other branches through judicial review, making sure they follow the Constitution.

DESIGN A NEW BRANCH OF GOVERNMENT

Create a name for it and decide what its
purpose and responsibilities would be.
Optional: Include the members of the branch.

_____

_____

_____

_____

_____

_____

_____

_____

_____

CITIZENSHIP

Citizenship means being a member of a country and having special rights and duties. Rights are like special powers that let us do things like speak freely or practice our religion. Responsibilities are like jobs we have to help our country, like following rules and helping others.

One way citizens can help their country is by voting. This means choosing leaders we think will make good decisions. We can also help by doing things in our neighborhood, like cleaning up or helping people who need it. Being a good citizen means using our rights wisely and doing our part to make our country a better place for everyone.

HOW CAN KIDS HELP?

- Volunteering: Kids can volunteer their time to help at local charities, animal shelters, or food banks. They can assist with tasks like sorting donations, feeding animals, or packing meals for those in need.

- Cleaning up: Kids can participate in community clean-up events to help keep parks, playgrounds, and streets clean and beautiful. They can pick up litter, plant flowers, or help maintain community gardens.

- Helping neighbors: Kids can lend a hand to elderly or disabled neighbors by offering to mow lawns, shovel snow, or run errands. They can also offer to walk pets or simply spend time chatting and providing companionship.

HOW CAN KIDS HELP?

- Fundraising: Kids can organize fundraisers at school or in their neighborhood to raise money for important causes, such as supporting local schools, funding medical research, or aiding disaster relief efforts.

- Advocating for change: Kids can raise awareness about issues that are important to them, such as environmental conservation or animal welfare, by writing letters to elected officials, organizing peaceful protests, or starting petition drives.

- Being a good role model: Kids can lead by example by demonstrating kindness, empathy, and respect towards others. They can stand up against bullying, include everyone in games and activities, and show appreciation for diversity and inclusion.

WAYS I CAN HELP

....

....

....

....

....

....

....

....

HOW CAN KIDS HELP?

Charity: an organization that helps a cause

Make up a charity!

- What will the charity be called?
- Who will the charity benefit?
- Will you raise money or supplies?
- How will you get the word out?

ALL ABOUT MY CHARITY

My name _____

Charity Name _____

Hometown _____

☐ Money   ☐ Materials

Raising money or materials for:

_____

_____

My Charity Logo

My Charity's Mission

Who or What Will Your
Charity Benefit?

My Feelings About

My Charity

THE CONSTITUTION

The Constitution is a very important document in our country. It was written a long time ago, when our country was just starting out. Think of it like the rules for a big club called the United States of America.

The Constitution has a few main parts. One part is called the Preamble. It's like the introduction to the Constitution. It talks about why the Constitution was written and what it aims to do.

Then, there are different sections, called articles. These articles talk about different things, like how the government works and what the rules are for the people in charge.

THE CONSTITUTION

The Constitution says that our government has three main parts: the executive branch, the legislative branch, and the judicial branch.

The Constitution also talks about the rights of the people. These are things like freedom of speech, freedom of religion, and the right to vote.

In summary, the Constitution is like the rulebook for our country. It tells us how the government works and what rights we have as citizens. It's a very important document that helps keep our country fair and free.

OPINION

Freedom of Speech means that we have the freedom to express our thoughts, ideas, and opinions without getting in trouble from the government. What message would you want to share with the world?

_____

_____

_____

_____

_____

_____

_____

_____

_____

_____

DECLARATION OF INDEPENDENCE

The Declaration of Independence is a very important document in our country's history. It was written a long time ago, in 1776, by a group of people who wanted to create a new country called the United States of America.

The Declaration of Independence starts by saying that all people are created equal. That means everyone should be treated fairly and with respect.

It then talks about some of the rights that people should have, like the right to life, liberty, and the pursuit of happiness. These are things that make us feel happy and fulfilled, like playing with friends, going to school, and being able to choose what we want to do with our lives.

DECLARATION OF INDEPENDENCE

The Declaration of Independence also talks about why the American colonies wanted to be independent from England. It says that the colonists felt like England was not treating them fairly and was not listening to their concerns. So, they decided to declare their independence and become their own country.

One of the most famous parts of the Declaration of Independence is the list of grievances, or complaints, against the King of England. These complaints include things like unfair taxes and not being able to have a say in the government.

In the end, the Declaration of Independence says that the American colonies are now free and independent states. It was a very brave thing for the colonists to do, and it laid the foundation for the country we live in today.

WE DECLARE...

"We want to be our own country!" The Declaration of Independence helped start the United States of America and gave people courage to fight for their rights and freedom. How or when do you show courage?

_____

_____

_____

_____

_____

_____

BILL OF RIGHTS

The Bill of Rights is a special list of rules that protects the rights of people in our country. It's like a set of promises made by our government to keep us safe and treat us fairly.

The Bill of Rights has ten rules, or amendments. These rules were added to the Constitution to make sure that everyone's rights are protected.

The amendment says that people have the freedom of speech. That means we can say what we think and feel without getting in trouble from the government.

The second amendment talks about the right to bear arms, which means the right to own guns for protection.

BILL OF RIGHTS

The third amendment says that soldiers can't stay in people's homes without their permission during peacetime.

The fourth amendment protects us from unfair searches and seizures. That means the police can't come into our homes or take our things without a good reason and a special permission called a warrant.

The fifth amendment says that people have the right to remain silent and not say anything that could get them in trouble. It also protects us from being treated unfairly by the government.

The other amendments in the Bill of Rights protect things like the right to a fair trial, the right to a lawyer, and the right to be treated fairly by the government.

WHAT CRAZY OR OUTRAGEOUS AMMENDMENTS WOULD YOU ADD TO THE BILL OF RIGHTS?

The Bill of Rights is like a set of rules that protect our freedoms and rights. It helps make sure that everyone is treated fairly and has the chance to live a happy and safe life. What rules would you add to the Bill of Rights?

1 _____

_____

2 _____

_____

3 _____

_____

THE PLEDGE OF ALLEGIENCE

The Pledge of Allegiance is a special promise that we say to show our love and loyalty to our country, the United States of America. It's like saying, "I promise to be a good citizen and support my country."

The Pledge of Allegiance goes like this:

"I pledge allegiance
to the flag
of the United States of America,
and to the republic
for which it stands,
one nation
under God,
indivisible,
with liberty
and justice for all."

THE PLEDGE OF ALLEGIENCE

Let's break it down:

- "I pledge allegiance" means "I promise to be loyal (show support) to."

- "To the flag" means the American flag.

- "Of the United States of America" tells us which country the flag represents.

- "And to the republic for which it stands" means we're promising to support our country, which is a republic where people vote for leaders.

- "One nation" reminds us that we're all part of the same country, even though we might be different in many ways.

THE PLEDGE OF ALLEGIENCE

- "Under God" is a way of saying that we believe in a higher power that helps guide us.

- "Indivisible" means that our country cannot be split apart or divided.

- "With liberty and justice for all" means that everyone in our country should be treated fairly and have the freedom to live their lives the way they choose.

When we say the Pledge of Allegiance, we stand up, face the flag, put our right hand over our heart, and say the words together with pride.

PLEDGE OF ALLEGIANCE

Saying the Pledge of Allegiance is a way for us to come together as one big family and show our respect for our country and the freedoms we enjoy. Re-write the Pledge of Allegiance or explain why it is important.

_____

_____

_____

_____

_____

_____

MY PLEDGE TO MYSELF

List ways you can show respect for yourself.

_____

_____

_____

_____

_____

_____

_____

GETTYSBURG ADDRESS

The Gettysburg Address is a famous speech that was given by President Abraham Lincoln during the Civil War. It's one of the most important speeches in American history.

President Lincoln gave the Gettysburg Address at a special ceremony in Gettysburg, Pennsylvania, where a big battle had taken place. Many people had fought and died there, and President Lincoln wanted to honor their memory.

In his speech, President Lincoln talked about the importance of freedom and equality for everyone. He said that our country was founded on the idea that all people are created equal and have the right to life, liberty, and the pursuit of happiness.

GETTYSBURG ADDRESS

President Lincoln also talked about the importance of coming together as a nation, even during difficult times. He said that the soldiers who fought and died at Gettysburg had given their lives so that our country could remain united and free.

The most famous part of the Gettysburg Address is the last sentence, where President Lincoln said: "that this nation, under God, shall have a new birth of freedom—and that government of the people, by the people, for the people, shall not perish from the earth."

In this sentence, President Lincoln is saying that he hopes our country will continue to be a place where freedom and democracy thrive, and where the government is made up of and works for the people.

GETTYSBURG ADDRESS

A speech that still inspires us today to work towards a better, more united nation. How can we be a better nation or place to live?

_____

_____

_____

_____

_____

_____

_____

_____

ARMED FORCES

The Armed Forces of the United States are like a big team of heroes who work together to protect our country and keep us safe. They are made up of brave men and women who are ready to defend our country at any time, in any place.

There are five main branches, or parts, of the Armed Forces:

The Army: The Army is like the ground force of the military. They use tanks, trucks, and helicopters to protect our country and help people in need, like during natural disasters.

The Navy: The Navy protects our country's waters and shores. They have big ships called aircraft carriers and submarines that can go underwater. They also have planes that can take off and land on the water.

ARMED FORCES

The Air Force: The Air Force protects our country's airspace. They have fighter jets and bombers that can fly very fast and very high. They also have special planes for things like refueling other planes in mid-air.

The Marines: The Marines are like the special forces of the military. They are trained to be tough and strong, and they can go anywhere in the world to protect our country and its interests.

The Coast Guard: The Coast Guard protects our country's coasts and helps people who are in trouble on the water. They have ships and boats that patrol the oceans and rescue swimmers and boaters who are in danger.

Each branch of the Armed Forces has its own special job, but they all work together to keep our country safe and free. We are very grateful for their service and bravery!

WHICH OF THE ARMED FORCES DO YOU THINK IS THE MOST IMPORTANT? WHY?

_____

_____

_____

_____

_____

_____

_____

_____

ARMED FORCES

LIST THE ARMED FORCES

ARMED FORCES
LIST THE ARMED FORCES

ARMY

NAVY

COAST
GUARD

AIRFORCE

MARINES

Write a letter to a person who have
served in the Armed Forces,
thanking them for their service.

_____ To

_____

_____

_____

_____

_____

_____

_____

_____

_____

From _____

_____

IMAGINE...

You are part of the American Government. Thinking of the three Branches of Government and the Armed Forces, which part of the American Government would you choose to work in? What appeals to you?

_____

_____

_____

_____

_____

_____

_____

_____

_____

_____

NATIONAL MONUMENTS

Washington, D.C. is home to many famous landmarks that are significant not only to the United States but also to the world. Here are some of the most notable landmarks:

The White House: The official residence and workplace of the President of the United States, located at 1600 Pennsylvania Avenue NW.

The U.S. Capitol: The seat of the United States Congress, where the House of Representatives and the Senate meet, located at Capitol Hill.

The Washington Monument: A towering obelisk built to honor George Washington, the first President of the United States, standing at 555 feet (169 meters) tall.

NATIONAL MONUMENTS

The Lincoln Memorial: A majestic monument dedicated to Abraham Lincoln, the 16th President of the United States, featuring a larger-than-life statue of Lincoln seated in contemplation.

The Jefferson Memorial: A memorial honoring Thomas Jefferson, the third President of the United States and the principal author of the Declaration of Independence, located on the Tidal Basin.

The Vietnam Veterans Memorial: A memorial dedicated to the men and women who served and sacrificed during the Vietnam War, featuring the names of over 58,000 fallen soldiers etched into black granite walls.

NATIONAL MONUMENTS

The Korean War Veterans Memorial: A solemn memorial honoring the veterans of the Korean War, featuring 19 stainless steel statues of soldiers representing different branches of the U.S. Armed Forces.

The Martin Luther King Jr. Memorial: A striking memorial dedicated to civil rights leader Martin Luther King Jr., featuring a 30-foot tall statue of King surrounded by walls inscribed with his famous quotes.

The National Mall: A vast, open green space stretching from the U.S. Capitol to the Lincoln Memorial, lined with museums, monuments, and memorials.

NATIONAL MONUMENTS

The Smithsonian Institution: A group of museums and research centers, including the National Air and Space Museum, the National Museum of American History, and the National Museum of Natural History, among others.

These are just a few of the many iconic landmarks that make Washington, D.C. such a unique and historically significant city. Each one tells a story and contributes to the rich tapestry of American history and culture.

Which National Monument do you think is the most influential?

_____

_____

The White House

The US Capitol

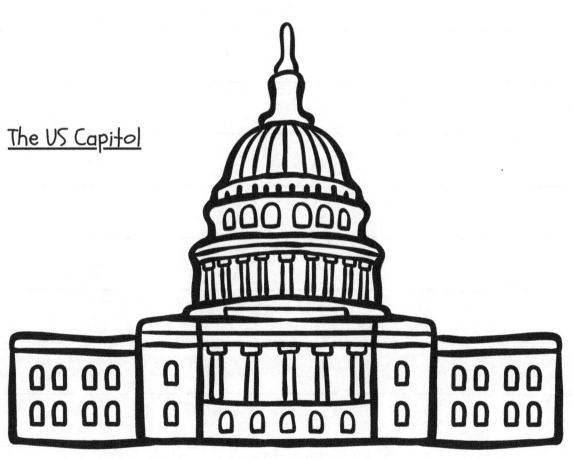

IMAGINE...

You were selected to create a NEW National Monument.
Which monument would you create? What is the significance
of the monument?

_____

_____

_____

_____

_____

_____

_____

_____

_____

_____

WHITE HOUSE FACTS

Construction: The White House, officially called the Executive Residence, was constructed between 1792 and 1800. It was designed by James Hoban, an Irish-born architect, and it is located in Washington, D.C.

Size: The White House has 132 rooms, including 35 bathrooms, 28 fireplaces, and 3 elevators. It also has a movie theater, bowling alley, and a tennis court.

Name Origin: The White House got its name after it was painted white to cover the fire damage it suffered during the War of 1812. Before that, it was known as the President's House or the Executive Mansion.

First Occupants: The first president to live in the White House was John Adams, the second president of the United States, along with his wife Abigail Adams. George Washington, the first president, did not live in the White House.

Oval Office: The Oval Office is the official office of the President of the United States. It was added to the White House in 1909 during President William Howard Taft's administration.

Tourist Destination: The White House is a popular tourist destination, attracting millions of visitors each year. While public tours are available, visitors must request tickets through their member of Congress in advance.

IMAGINE...

You get to design a brand new room for the White House.
What would be the theme of your room? What would you
include in your room?

_____

_____

_____

_____

_____

_____

_____

_____

_____

_____

NEW ROOM IN THE WHITE HOUSE

Create the floor plan of your new room for the White House. What will be included? Draw it here.

White House Sleepover

You are invited to spend the night at the White House, but little do you know, it's no ordinary sleepover – it's an adventure-filled quest to uncover the secrets hidden within the vast halls and mysterious passages of the White House! As you explore the grand rooms and corridors of the White House, you stumble upon a hidden door behind a bookshelf in the Oval Office. Intrigued, you and your friends decide to venture inside, only to find yourselves transported to a magical world filled with enchanted creatures and ancient treasures!

White House
Sleepover Continued

The Superhero President

Imagine you wake up one morning to discover that you've been magically transformed into the President of the United States! But here's the twist – you're not just any president; you're a superhero president with incredible powers! What powers will you have and how will you save the country? So put on your superhero cape, grab your trusty animal sidekicks, and get ready for the most outrageous adventure of your life as the superhero president of the United States!

_____

_____

_____

_____

_____

_____

_____

_____

The Superhero President

_____

_____

_____

_____

_____

_____

_____

_____

_____

_____

Reader's Theater
The Birth of Our Constitution

Characters: Narrator | Benjamin Franklin
James Madison | Thomas Jefferson
George Washington | Abigail Adams

Scene – Narrator:	A meeting room in Philadelphia in 1787. Delegates are gathered to draft the United States Constitution

Narrator:	Welcome to "The Birth of Our Constitution." Our story begins in the summer of 1787 in Philadelphia, where delegates from across the land gathered to create a document that would shape our nation.
James Madison:	Friends, we are here to forge a new path for our young nation. Let us create a Constitution that unites us all.
George Washington:	I agree, James. We must build a strong foundation that makes sure there is justice and freedom for all.

Reader's Theater
The Birth of Our Constitution

Benjamin Franklin: Aye, let us learn from our past mistakes and create a government that stands the test of time.

Narrator: As the delegates worked tirelessly, they faced challenges and debates, but with perseverance and compromise, they crafted the United States Constitution.

Thomas Jefferson: James, our Constitution must protect the rights of the people. How can we ensure their voices are heard?

James Madison: Perhaps a system of checks and balances, Thomas. Three branches of government – legislative, executive, and judicial – working together to prevent any one from becoming too powerful.

Abigail Adams: It's important for us to remember that even though women aren't present in this room, their voices matter. We must strive for equality and justice for all.

Reader's Theater
The Birth of Our Constitution

George Washington: We do need to protect the rights of the people and having three branches of government will help to make sure each branch has some power.

Benjamin Franklin: I do think this is a plan that can work to create a successful government for our country.

Thomas Jefferson: I agree with all of you. Let's get this constitution written for the people!

Narrator: The delegates debated and compromised, shaping the Constitution with the wisdom of ages and the hopes of a new nation.

Abigail Adams: I think all people will be happy with the constitution to protect the rights of all.

Reader's Theater
The Birth of Our Constitution

Narrator: And so, on September 17, 1787, the delegates signed the United States Constitution, a beacon of democracy for generations to come.

All Delegates: Hip, hip, hooray! Hip, hip, hooray!

Narrator: Let us remember the lessons of those who came before us, for it is through unity and understanding that we continue to build a better union.

Reader's Theater
Our Constitution, Our Rights

Characters:	Sarah	Mrs. Johnson
	Alex	Narrator
	Thomas	

Scene – Narrator:	Welcome to "Our Constitution, Our Rights," a play that explores how the Constitution relates to each of you!
Mrs. Johnson:	Today, we're going to learn about the Constitution of the United States. It's not just an old document; it's something that affects all of us in our daily lives.
Sarah:	But how does the Constitution relate to us, Ms. Johnson?
Mrs. Johnson:	That's a great question, Sarah! The Constitution is like a rulebook for our country. It tells us what our rights are and how our government works.

Reader's Theater
Our Constitution, Our Rights

Alex:	So, does that mean we have rights, too?
Mrs. Johnson:	Yes, Alex! The Constitution guarantees certain rights to all Americans, including kids like you. For example, you have the right to speak your mind and the right to be treated fairly by the law.
Sarah:	Wow, I never knew that!
Narrator:	As Ms. Johnson continued to explain, the students began to realize just how important the Constitution is in their everyday lives.
Alex:	But what if someone tries to take away our rights?
Sarah:	That's where the Constitution comes in, Alex. It's like our guardian angel, protecting us and making sure our rights are always protected.

Reader's Theater
Our Constitution, Our Rights

Narrator: Suddenly, the classroom door opens, and Thomas enters.

Thomas: Hey, everyone! Did you know that we can also change the Constitution if we think something needs to be different?

Mrs. Johnson: That's right, Thomas! The Constitution can be amended, or changed, to better meet the needs of our country. It's a living document that grows and changes with us.

Thomas: I'm not sure what I would change now, but it's good to know that we can make changes if we need to.

Narrator: The Constitution is not just a piece of history. It's a living document that shapes our lives and protects our rights every single day.

Reader's Theater
The Bill of Rights Explained

Characters:	Emma	Thomas
	Liam	Narrator
	Mrs. Anderson	

Scene – Narrator:	A colorful classroom with posters on the walls and artwork hanging all around. Students are seated, eager to learn about the Bill of Rights.

Narrator:	Today, we embark on a journey to discover the treasures of our Constitution's first ten amendments, known as the Bill of Rights.
Mrs. Anderson:	Good morning, class! Today, we're going to learn about the Bill of Rights, which gives us many important freedoms and protections.
Emma:	Mrs. Anderson, what are the Bill of Rights?

Reader's Theater
The Bill of Rights Explained

Mrs. Anderson:	That's a fantastic question, Emma! The Bill of Rights is like a superhero cape for our rights. It's a list of ten special rules that make sure the government respects our freedoms.
Liam:	Wow, like what kind of freedoms?
Mrs. Anderson:	Well, Liam, let's find out together! Who wants to help me explain the first amendment?
Emma:	I'll give it a try! The first amendment gives us five awesome freedoms: freedom of speech, freedom of religion, freedom of the press, the right to assemble peacefully, and the right to petition the government.
Mrs. Anderson:	That's correct, Emma! And why do you think these freedoms are important?

Reader's Theater
The Bill of Rights Explained

Emma: Because they let us express ourselves, believe what we want, and tell the truth without being afraid.

Narrator: As the class continued to explore the Bill of Rights, they discovered the importance of each amendment in protecting their freedoms and making sure there is justice for all.

Liam: Hey, Emma, what's the second amendment all about?

Emma: The second amendment is like our right to have a superhero shield! It protects our right to own guns responsibly.

Thomas: That makes me feel safer. Did you know that the Bill of Rights also guarantees our right to a fair trial and protects us from cruel and unusual punishment?

Reader's Theater
The Bill of Rights Explained

Mrs. Johnson:	That's right, Thomas! The Bill of Rights is all about making sure we're treated fairly and with respect by our government.
Narrator:	As the class continued to explore the Bill of Rights, they discovered the importance of each amendment in protecting their freedoms and making sure there is justice for all.

Reader's Theater
The Declaration of Independence:
A Story of Freedom

Characters:	Thomas Jefferson	Abigail Adams
Narrator	John Adams	George Washington
	Benjamin Franklin	

Scene – Narrator:	A meeting room in Philadelphia in 1776. Delegates are gathered to discuss the Declaration of Independence.

Narrator:	Welcome to "The Declaration of Independence: A Story of Freedom." Join us as we journey back to the summer of 1776, where brave men gathered to declare independence from British rule.
Thomas Jefferson:	Friends, the time has come for us to break free and declare our independence. We hold these truths to be self-evident, that all men are created equal...
John Adams:	Indeed, Thomas. We must assert our unalienable rights to life, liberty, and the pursuit of happiness.

Reader's Theater
The Declaration of Independence:
A Story of Freedom

Benjamin Franklin: Let us write a declaration that will inspire future generations to stand up for their freedoms.

Thomas Jefferson: Every person should have freedom and rights as citizens.

John Adams: I agree Mr. Jefferson. Every person deserves to be free and happy.

Narrator: As the delegates worked tirelessly, they wrote the Declaration of Independence, a document that would change the course of history.

Thomas Jefferson: The Declaration of Independence makes sure that all men are created equal.

Reader's Theater

The Declaration of Independence:
A Story of Freedom

Abigail Adams:	All men? What about the women in the country? Women are an important part of our nation.
George Washington:	You are right, Abigail. Women were not written into the orginal Declaration of Independence, but are very important, indeed.
Abigail Adams:	While the men are inside discussing independence, let us not forget the important role women play in the fight for freedom. We may not have a voice in the room, but our actions speak volumes.
George Washington:	Women like you are the backbone of our nation, supporting us in our darkest hours.
Narrator:	Suddenly, the doors burst open, and the delegates emerge, holding the Declaration of Independence high.

Reader's Theater
The Declaration of Independence:
A Story of Freedom

Thomas Jefferson: We hold these truths to be self-evident, that all men are created equal...

Abigail Adams: And women too! Don't forget, we work hard to support the nation.

John Adams: You are right, Abigail. Women should have been written into the original Declaration of Independence.

Narrator: And so, on July 4, 1776, the Declaration of Independence was adopted, proclaiming to the world that the thirteen colonies were now free and independent states.

George Washington: Remember the courage and sacrifice of those who came before us. It was because of their bravery that we enjoy the freedoms we hold dear today.

Reader's Theater
Journey Through the
Three Branches of Government

Characters:	Mr. Johnson	Executive Branch
Narrator	Lily	Judicial Branch
	Max	Legislative Branch

Scene – Narrator:	A classroom decorated with posters about government. Students are seated, eager to learn about the three branches.

Narrator:	Welcome, thank you for joining us as we go on a journey to discover how our government works.
Mr. Johnson:	Good morning, class! Today, we're going to learn about the three branches of government: the legislative, executive, and judicial branches. They work together like a well-oiled machine to keep our country running smoothly.
Lily:	But what do each of the branches do?

Reader's Theater
Journey Through the
Three Branches of Government

Mr. Johnson: That's a great question, Lily! Let's find out together.

Legislative Branch: Hi learners! Welcome to the Legislative Branch, also known as Congress. We're like the lawmakers of the land, creating laws to help our country grow and prosper.

Max: Wow, that's so cool! How do you make laws?

Legislative Branch: Well, it all starts with a bill. A bill is an idea for a new law. We debate and discuss the bill, and if enough of us agree, it becomes a law that everyone must follow.

Max: It seems like a lot of people work together.

Legislative Branch: You are right, Max. It takes a team of people to process a bill into a law.

Reader's Theater
Journey Through the
Three Branches of Government

Executive Branch:	Hello, students! Welcome to the Executive Branch, led by the President. We're like the managers of the country, making sure the laws are carried out to keep our nation safe and strong.
Lily:	That sounds important! What does the President do?
Executive Branch:	The President signs bills into law, commands the military, and represents our country to the world. They're like the captain of a ship, guiding us through calm seas and stormy waters.
Max:	It would be amazing to be the President of the United States. It's good to know they are not alone to lead the country.

Reader's Theater
Journey Through the
Three Branches of Government

Judicial Branch: Greetings, kids! Welcome to the Judicial Branch, led by the Supreme Court. We're like the referees of the nation, making sure the laws are fair and everyone is treated equally.

Max: How do you do that?

Judicial Branch: We read the laws to understand them, then decide if they're being followed correctly. If someone breaks the law, we make sure they're held accountable and receive a fair trial.

Lily: Is that why Judicial sounds like judge? A judge oversees the fair trial, right?

Mr. Johnson: You got it, Lily! Let us remember the importance of the three branches of government in keeping our country strong and free.

Made in the USA
Monee, IL
03 January 2025

75920300R00057